Calculations

Katherine Pate

Contents

Acknowledgements

All images and illustrations are © Shutterstock.com and © HarperCollins*Publishers*.

Every effort has been made to trace copyright holders and obtain their permission for the use of copyright material. The author and publisher will gladly receive information enabling them to rectify any error or omission in subsequent editions. All facts are correct at time of going to press.

Published by Collins
An imprint of HarperCollins*Publishers* Ltd
1 London Bridge Street
London SE1 9GF

© HarperCollins*Publishers* Limited

ISBN 9780008259518

First published 2017

10 9 8 7 6 5 4 3 2

All rights reserved. No part of this publication may be reproduced, stored in a retrieval system, or transmitted, in any form or by any means, electronic, mechanical, photocopying, recording or otherwise, without the prior permission of Collins.

British Library Cataloguing in Publication Data.

A CIP record of this book is available from the British Library.

Commissioning Editor: Michelle I'Anson
Author: Katherine Pate
Project Manager and Editorial: Rebecca Skinner
Cover Design: Paul Oates
Inside Concept Design: Paul Oates
Text Design and Layout: Q2A Media
Printed in China by RR Donnelley APS

How to use this book

- You will need a blue / black pen or a dark pencil and a ruler (showing centimetres and millimetres).

- You **may not** use a calculator to answer any of the questions.

- Complete one test at a time. Test 1 is easier than the KS2 SAT papers. Tests 2 to 5 are the same level of difficulty as the actual tests and Test 6 is more challenging.

- Follow the instructions for each question.

- Questions are worth 1, 2 or 3 marks. The number under each line at the side of the page tells you the maximum number of marks for each question part.

- If you need to do working out, you can use the space around the question.

- Some questions have a 'Show your method' grid. For these questions, you may get a mark for showing your method even if the final answer is wrong.

- Cross out any answers that you wish to change.

- Remember to check your work carefully.

- The answers are in the pull-out section at the centre of this book.

- After completing all the tests, fill in the progress chart to identify what you are doing well in and what you can improve.

1. Ben uses each of these cards once to make a 3-digit number.

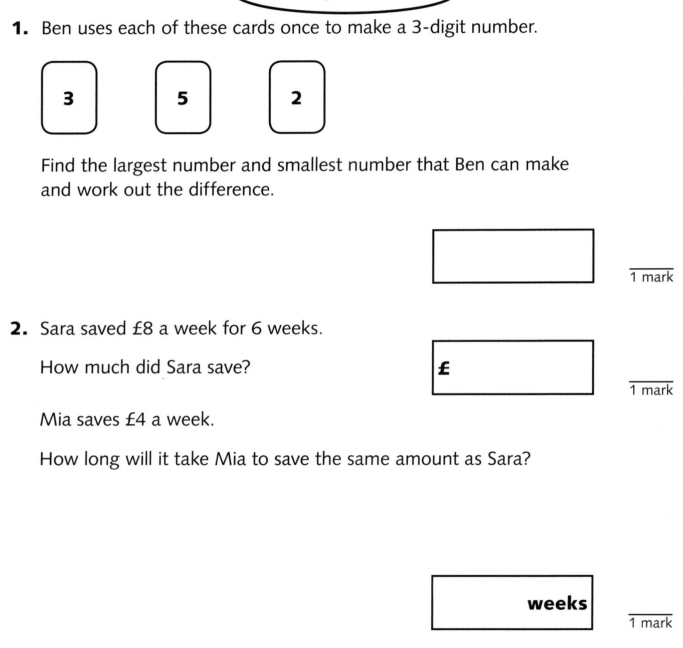

| 3 | 5 | 2 |

Find the largest number and smallest number that Ben can make and work out the difference.

1 mark

2. Sara saved £8 a week for 6 weeks.

How much did Sara save?

£

1 mark

Mia saves £4 a week.

How long will it take Mia to save the same amount as Sara?

weeks

1 mark

3. Write the missing numbers.

42 is ☐ times greater than 7

72 is ☐ times greater than 9

12 is ☐ times smaller than 48

2 marks

4. Chan has £6.52
His mum gives him £5
He pays £1.75 for his bus fare and £7.20 for a cinema ticket.

Show that Chan has enough money left to buy popcorn.

£2.50

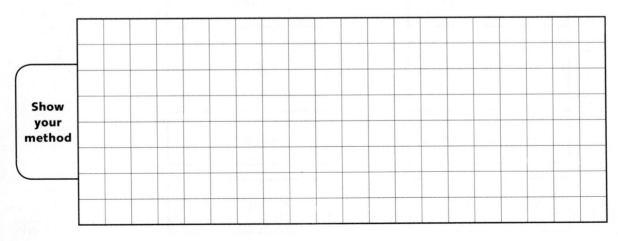

Show your method

2 marks

5. A teacher buys 28 books.
Each book costs £4.95

Complete the sentence.

28 to the nearest ten is ☐ and £4.95 to the nearest pound is £

Use your rounded numbers to calculate an estimate for the total cost of the books.

£

1 mark

6. Match each calculation to the correct result.

One has been done for you.

146.2 ÷ 10	1,462
146.2 × 100	14.62
1.462 × 1,000	14,620
146.2 ÷ 100	1.462

2 marks

7. Shivi says,

'You cannot divide 13 people into equal groups of more than 1 or less than 13.'

Shivi is correct.

Explain how you know.

_____

1 mark

8. Write the three missing digits to make this **subtraction** correct.

$$
\begin{array}{cccc}
6 & 3 & \boxed{} & 7 \\
-\;\boxed{} & 5 & 1 & \boxed{} \\
\hline
4 & 8 & 3 & 5 \\
\end{array}
$$

2 marks

1. Nathan runs 724 metres and stops for a rest.
He then runs a further 619 metres.

How many metres does Nathan run in total?

m

1 mark

2. Sahil has £700
He buys a laptop,
a monitor and a printer.

£373.99   £149.79   £85

How much money does Sahil have left?

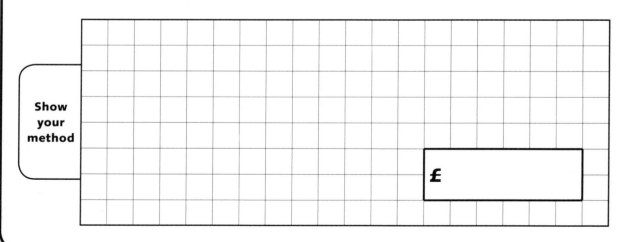

Show your method

£

2 marks

3. Lola needs to work out the answer to this subtraction.

5,072 – 249

First she estimates the answer.

Tick the best calculation for her estimate.

5,000 – 300   5,000 – 200

Lola calculates the exact answer to be 4,857

Complete this calculation to check her answer.

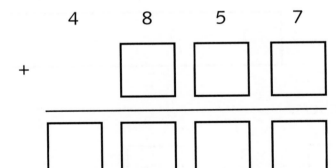

```
        4   8   5   7
  +        □   □   □
     _____
       □   □   □   □
```

Is Lola's answer of 4,857 correct?

yes □   no □

4. It takes a teacher **seven** minutes to mark **one** test.

How long will it take to mark 22 tests?

 hours minutes

2 marks

5. Write **all** the common multiples of 3 and 5 that are **greater than 50** and **less than 100**

2 marks

6. Write the missing numbers.

128 $\xrightarrow{\div 8}$ ☐ $\xrightarrow{\times 3}$ ☐

1 mark

339 $\xrightarrow{-287}$ ☐ $\xrightarrow{\div 4}$ ☐

1 mark

7. An airline pilot flies from London to Istanbul and back again.
The pilot does this 14 times a month.
The distance from London to Istanbul is 2,516 km.

How far does the pilot fly each month?

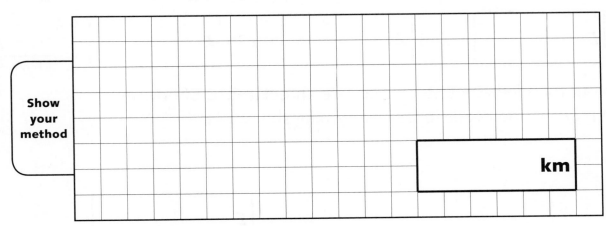

Show your method

km

2 marks

8. Kara says, *'34 is a factor of 2,108'*

Explain why she is correct.

_____

_____

1 mark

1. Jade is given £100 for her birthday.
She wants to spend it on a riding lesson (£32), a new coat (£48) and a game (£25).

Round each amount to the nearest £10

£32 £ [   ]   £48 £ [   ]   £25 £ [   ]

1 mark

Use your rounded amounts to calculate an **estimate** of how much more money Jade needs to buy everything she wants.

£ [   ]

1 mark

2. Write the missing digits to make this **multiplication** correct.

```
        2   7
  ×        [ ]
  _____
      2  [ ] 6
```

1 mark

3. Write the missing digits to make this **subtraction** correct.

$$
\begin{array}{ccccc}
 & 1 & \square & 2 & \square & 7 \\
- & & 3 & \square & 1 & \square \\
\hline
 & 1 & 0 & 8 & 7 & 9 \\
\end{array}
$$

2 marks

4. One train carriage has 64 seats.
240 people get on a train with **three** carriages.

How many people do **not** have a seat?

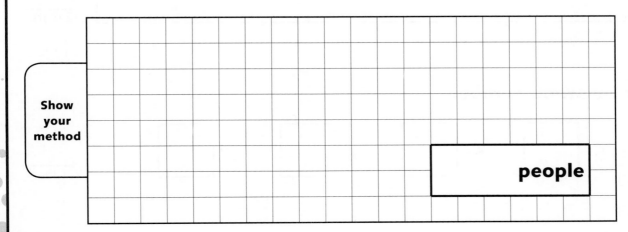

Show your method

people

2 marks

5. Raji is having a birthday party.
There will be 8 people at the party including Raji.
They are having pizza and going bowling.

Pizza
£4.50 each

Bowling
£6 each

Work out the total cost.

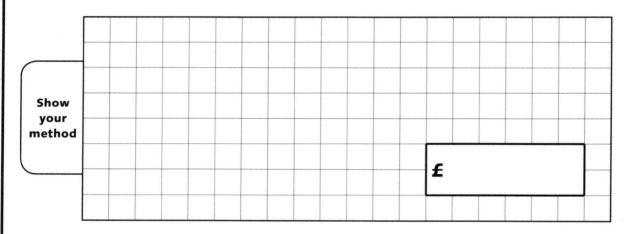

Show your method

£

2 marks

6. Tick the **prime number**.

51 ☐   53 ☐   55 ☐   57 ☐

1 mark

Answers

For 2-mark answers shown with a star (2*), award 2 marks for the correct answer.
If the answer is incorrect, award 1 mark for an appropriate method.

Question	Answer(s)	Mark(s)	Content domain(s)
	Test 1		
1	297	1	3C4, 3N3
2	£48 12 weeks	1 1 (1 mark for a correct calculation using the pupil's answer to the first part of the question)	4C6a, 4C8
3	6 8 4	2 (1 mark for two correct)	4C6a
4	£2.57 seen	2*	5C4, 5M9a
5	30 AND 5 £150	1 1	5C3, 4N4b
6	146.2 × 100 = 14,620 1.462 × 1000 = 1,462 146.2 ÷ 100 = 1.462	2 (1 mark for two correct)	5C6b
7	Answers will vary, e.g. *13 is a prime number. /* *13 cannot be divided by any numbers* *except for 1 and itself.* Accept an appropriate diagram.	1	5C5b
8	6 3 **4** 7 − **1** 5 1 **2** 4 8 3 5	2 (1 mark for two correct)	4C2
	Test 2		
1	1,343 m	1	3C2

2	£91.22	2*	5C4, 5C2, 5M9a
3	5,000 – 200 $\begin{array}{ccccc} & 4 & 8 & 5 & 7 \\ + & & 2 & 4 & 9 \\ \hline & 5 & 1 & 0 & 6 \end{array}$ AND 'no'	1 1	4C2, 5C3
4	2 hours 34 minutes	2 (1 mark for 154 minutes)	4C7, 5M4
5	60, 75, 90	2 (1 mark for two correct)	6C5
6	16 AND 48 52 AND 13	1 1	6C6, 6C8
7	70,448 km	2*	6C7a
8	Answers will vary, e.g. e.g. *2,108 divided by 34 gives an answer of 62 (a whole number).*	1	6C7b, 6C7c
Test 3			
1	£30 AND £50 AND £30 £10	1 1	5C3, 4C4, 4N4b
2	$\begin{array}{ccc} & 2 & 7 \\ \times & & 8 \\ \hline 2 & 1 & 6 \end{array}$	1	4C7
3	$\begin{array}{ccccc} 1 & 4 & 2 & 9 & 7 \\ - & 3 & 4 & 1 & 8 \\ \hline 1 & 0 & 8 & 7 & 9 \end{array}$	2 (1 mark for three correct)	5C2
4	48 people	2*	5C7b, 5C8b
5	£84	2*	6C8, 5M9a
6	53	1	5C5c
7	1, 2, 4	2 (1 mark for two correct)	5C5a

8	64 boxes	2* (1 mark if answer is incorrect but 64.75 OR $64\frac{3}{4}$ is seen)	6C7b, 6C7c
Test 4			
1	£3.45 AND £5 £1.55	1 1	3C2, 5M9a
2	£194.25	1	5C7a, 5M9a
3	8 combinations	1	4C8
4	36	1	5C8a
5	38 Answer will vary, e.g. *James added 3 + 7 first instead of multiplying 7 × 5.*	1 1	6C9
6	20 × 1,200 = 24,000 OR 20 × 1,000 = 20,000	1 1 OR 1 1	6C3
7	15 boxes	2* (1 mark if answer is incorrect but 14.25 OR $14\frac{1}{4}$ is seen)	6C7b
8	41, 43, 47	2 (1 mark for two correct)	6C5
Test 5			
1	51 metres	1	3C7, 3M7
2	218 people	2*	4C4
3	5 3 8, 4	2 (1 mark for three correct)	5C5d

4	$8 \times 7 + 6 = 62$ $96 \div 12 - 3 = 5$	1 1	5C8b
5	Answers will vary, e.g. *578 divided by 32 does not give a whole number (18 r2).*	1	6C7b
6	£5.45	3 (2 marks for an appropriate method with no more than one arithmetic error OR 1 mark for evidence of an appropriate method)	6C8, 5M9a
7	52 seen £389,948 seen AND 'no'	1 1	6C7a
Test 6			
1	An explanation that shows Simone has four times as many sweets as Maya, e.g. *4 × 16 (64) is 4 times as many as 2 × 8 (16) /* $64 \div 16 = \frac{4}{16} \times 4 = 64$	1 (Do not accept vague or incomplete explanations)	4C8
2	£397	1	6C7b
3	23.5 OR $23\frac{1}{2}$ minutes	1	6C7b, 5C8c, 5M9d
4	£71,204	1	6C7a
5	From top to bottom: 72, 6 From top to bottom: 35 and 30, 7	1 1	6C8
6	**4** + 6 ÷ **3** – **5** (division must be performed first)	1	6C9
7	less than Answers will vary, e.g. *3,000 is less than 3,087 and 50 is greater than 49, so the result is smaller.*	1 1	6C3
8	9	1	6C5

7. Write down **all** the common factors of 8 and 20

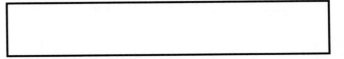

$\overline{\text{2 marks}}$

8. There are 16 lollies in a box.
A shop sells 1,036 lollies in one week.

How many **whole boxes** of lollies is this?

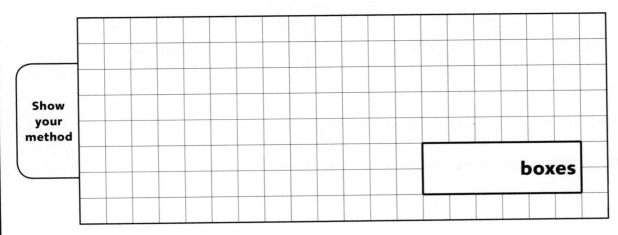

Show your method

boxes

$\overline{\text{2 marks}}$

1. Dan buys some felt-tip pens.
He works out his change using the calculation below.

$$
\begin{array}{r}
5\ .\ 0\ \ 0 \\
-\ 3\ .\ 4\ \ 5 \\
\hline
\end{array}
$$

Complete the sentences.

The cost of the felt-tip pens is £ [   ]

Dan paid with a £ [   ] note and got £ [   ] change.

2 marks

2. A hotel room costs £64.75 for one night.

Work out the cost of the hotel room for three nights.

£ [   ]

1 mark

3. A shop sells **four** different types of sandwich:

egg   ham   chicken   tuna

It also sells **two** different types of soup:

tomato   lentil

How many combinations of soup and sandwich are there?

combinations

1 mark

4. Here are some numbers in a box.

27		36		20
	3		19	49

Write down a number from the box that is a multiple of 9 **and** a square number.

1 mark

5. Here is a calculation.

$3 + 7 \times 5$

James says that the answer to the calculation is 50

James is **wrong**.

Work out the correct answer.

$\boxed{}$

Explain the mistake that James made.

_____

_____

6. Soraya needs to work out $22 \times 1{,}159$

Write a calculation she could use to **estimate** the answer.

$\boxed{}$ × $\boxed{}$

Work out the estimate.

$\boxed{}$

7. A school gives a medal to each pupil on Sports Day.
Medals come in boxes of 24
There are 342 pupils in the school.

How many boxes of medals does the school need to buy?

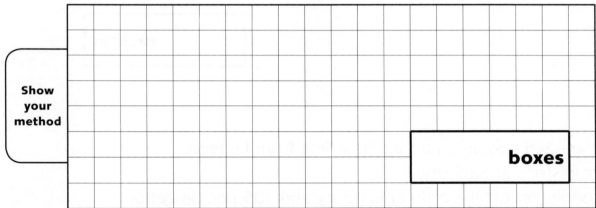

Show your method

boxes

2 marks

8. Write down **all** the prime numbers between 40 and 50

2 marks

How am I doing?   Score   **/13**

1. A garden fence is made from 17 panels.
Each panel is 3 metres long.

Work out the total length of the fence.

	metres

1 mark

2. There are 245 people on a train travelling from London.
The train stops at Banbury.
132 people get off the train at Banbury and 105 people get on.
The next stop is Birmingham.

How many people are on the train when it arrives at Birmingham?

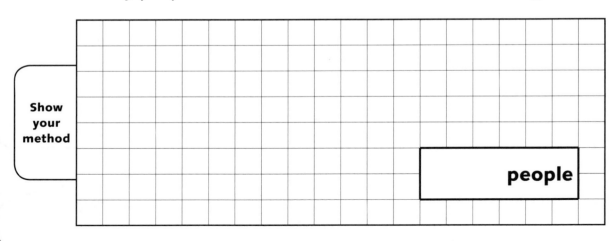

Show your method

	people

2 marks

3. Write the missing numbers.

$$\boxed{}^{2} = 25$$

$$27 = \boxed{}^{3}$$

$$\boxed{}^{2} = 64 = \boxed{}^{3}$$

2 marks

4. Write ×, +, − or ÷ in each box to make the calculations correct.

$$8 \ \boxed{} \ 7 \ \boxed{} \ 6 = 62$$

1 mark

$$96 \ \boxed{} \ 12 \ \boxed{} \ 3 = 5$$

1 mark

5. Sujit says, *'32 is not a factor of 578'*

Explain why he is correct.

_____

_____
1 mark

6. Amelia is making fudge to sell at the school fair.

Sugar costs 79 p per kg.
Butter costs £1.19 for 250 g.
Cream costs £2.98 per litre.

Amelia uses 2 kg of sugar, 500 g of butter and $\frac{1}{2}$ a litre of cream.

Calculate the total cost.

Show your method

£

3 marks

7. A garage sells cars.
Its target is to sell £500,000 worth
of cars every three months.

The garage sells 13 of these cars in
January, 16 in February and 23 in March.

Does the garage meet its target?

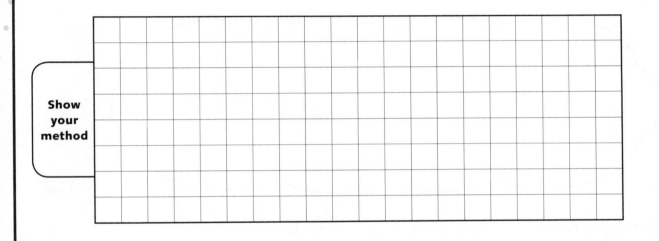

Show your method

yes ☐   no ☐

2 marks

1. Simone buys **4** bags of humbugs.
Maya buys **2** bags of bonbons.

Simone says, *'I have four times as many sweets as Maya.'*

Explain why Simone is correct.

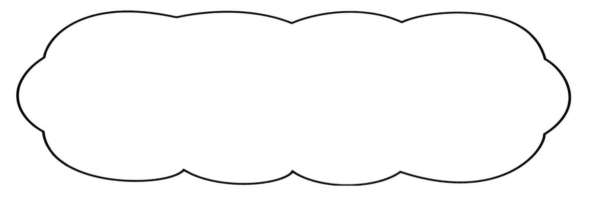

1 mark

2. 24 people share £9,528 of prize money equally.

How much does each person get?

£

1 mark

3. David fills a paddling pool using a hosepipe.
Water runs into the paddling pool through the hosepipe at a rate of
12 litres per minute.

How long will it take to fill the pool with 282 litres of water?

| minutes |

4. 2,543 people pay £28 each for a theatre ticket.

What is the total amount paid for theatre tickets?

£ [   ]

5. Complete these multiplication walls.
Work out the product of two bricks next to each other and write it on the brick above.

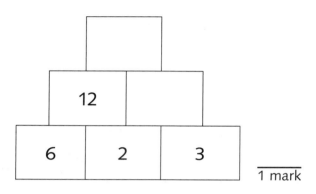

1 mark

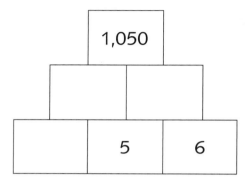

1 mark

6. Here are some number cards.

3	4	5

Use each card once in the calculation below to give an answer of 1

☐ + 6 ÷ ☐ − ☐ = 1

1 mark

7. Cherie wants to work out 3,087 ÷ 49
She estimates the answer by calculating 3,000 ÷ 50

Is her estimate **greater than** or **less than** the exact answer to 3,087 ÷ 49?

greater than ☐   less than ☐

Explain how you know.

_____

_____

8. What is the **highest common factor** of 36, 54 and 171?

How am I doing? ☺ ☺ ☹   Score   /10

Pupil progress chart

Skills	✓ or X
I can add and subtract in my head.	
I can add and subtract using written methods.	
I can estimate answers and use inverse operations to check my answers.	
I can add and subtract to solve problems.	
I can recognise and find different types of number: multiples, factors, primes, squares and cubes.	
I can multiply and divide in my head.	
I can multiply and divide using written methods.	
I can solve different types of problems using all four operations.	
I can carry out operations in the correct order.	

What am I doing well in?

_____

_____

What do I need to improve?

_____

_____